First published in Great Britain in 2003 by Brimax™,
an imprint of Octopus Publishing Group Ltd
2-4 Heron Quays, London E14 4JP

 Children's Publishing

This edition published in the United States of America in 2003 by
Peter Bedrick Books,
an imprint of McGraw-Hill Children's Publishing,
a Division of The McGraw-Hill Companies
8787 Orion Place
Columbus, Ohio 43240-4027

www.MHkids.com

Printed in China.

1-57768-508-3

1 2 3 4 5 6 7 8 9 10 BRI 09 08 07 06 05 04 03 02

Gods and Goddesses from Greek Myths

Retold by Pat Posner

Illustrated by Olwyn Whelan

PETER BEDRICK BOOKS

Columbus, Ohio

Introduction

Thousands of years ago, the people of ancient Greece worshiped gods and goddesses who had superhuman strengths and powers. These gods and goddesses could cover vast distances in the blink of an eye, transform themselves into other creatures, and were immortal. They also had very human faults and flaws, such as jealousy, anger, and greed.

The stories in this book tell of the Greek gods and goddesses from their creation to their marriages, feuds, and rivalries. The stories also feature nymphs, dragons, and other magical creatures. And let's not forget mere mortals. Greek gods and goddesses liked nothing better than to meddle in the lives of human beings. Sometimes the gods and goddesses showed kindness to mortals, and even fell in love with them. Other times they were spiteful and caused mortals harm.

Traveling storytellers shared stories about gods and goddesses, called myths, as they journeyed all over ancient Greece. There is no one correct version of the myths because these stories evolved over time, as they were passed down verbally from generation to generation. However, several important pieces of literature on ancient Greece did emerge to help immortalize the myths. Homer's epic poems *The Iliad* and *The Odyssey*, Hesiod's *Theogony*, and Ovid's *Metamorphoses* all focus on the basic characters and themes of Greek mythology. Historians also learned about these stories by studying ancient vases, temple carvings, and other artifacts that told these stories in pictures.

The myths probably were also a way to help the ancient Greeks understand nature. When it thundered outside, the ancient Greeks thought that the gods on Mount Olympus were angry. Even though we now have scientific explanations for most natural phenomena, the myths of the ancient Greeks are still exciting to read. They are classic literature and the basis and inspiration for many of the world's great poems and novels. Knowledge of these myths is also important in appreciating and understanding history and literature.

Contents

Zeus and the Olympians

Long ago, the Titan gods ruled the heavens, and Cronus was their king. He and his wife, Rhea, had five children. Because Cronus had been warned by a fortune teller that one of his children would imprison him in the Underworld, he swallowed each child just after it was born.

"No child of mine shall live!" he shouted. "Not on earth or in the sky or in the sea!"

When Rhea had her sixth baby, she named him Zeus and hid him in a cave on the island of Crete. She did not want Cronus to eat her baby boy, so she wrapped a stone in baby clothes and went to find Cronus. Thinking that his wife was holding their baby, Cronus snatched the bundled rock from her and swallowed it.

Baby Zeus was safe, rocking in a cradle that hung from the mouth of the cave over the sea. Rhea was scared that Cronus might hear Zeus crying and kill him by swallowing him, so she came up with a solution. She taught some young Cretans how to do a sword-dance. Every time Zeus began to cry, the Cretans danced, and the sound of their swords clashing against their shields drowned out the baby's wails. The Cretans took good care of Zeus, feeding him goat's milk.

Mountain nymphs, beautiful nature spirits, brought food for Zeus, too. He grew quickly and became very strong. When he was fully grown, the nymphs told him his father had swallowed Zeus' brothers and sisters when they were babies.

"I will go and find him," vowed Zeus. "I will fight him and the Titans, and then I will become the ruler of the sky and king of all the gods."

The nymphs gave Zeus a magic herb to put in Cronus's cup of nectar. Zeus did as they instructed. Cronus drank the nectar, and coughed out his children—Hades, Poseidon, Hera, Hestia, and Demeter—all fully grown. They, too, wanted revenge on their father and agreed to help Zeus fight the Titans. Cronus also coughed out the stone

that he had thought was baby Zeus.

"After we have won the war, I will set this stone at the center of the world," said Zeus.

Zeus and his followers set up camp on Mount Olympus and the war began. One day, Zeus went to find his grandmother, Gaia, to ask her advice on how to win the war. Gaia was the spirit of the earth, and Zeus knew that she did not approve of the things that Cronus

had done. He hoped that she would be able to help him.

"Long ago," Gaia told Zeus, "when Uranus was ruler of the sky and king of the Titans, he threw six of our sons into the Underworld. Three of them, who each have fifty heads and a hundred hands, are locked in a prison and guarded by a fearful, many-headed dragon. The other three, each with only one eye, are the Cyclopes. They are imprisoned even deeper in the Underworld and bound with metal shackles." She finished her story by saying, "If you can set all six free, you will win the war."

Gaia gave Zeus a special sickle to help him kill the dragon. Then Zeus set off for the Underworld, the dreadful land beneath the earth where the dead lived. Making his way through the murky gloom, he came to the prison. The dragon Gaia had told him about was terrible. It had snarling heads, writhing snakes for legs, and a scorpion for a tail. The horrible beast guarded the gates that surrounded the prison.

Every time the dragon flew at Zeus, Zeus slashed at it with the sickle. Soon, the dragon fell to the ground dead.

Zeus freed the three prisoners and took them to Mount Olympus. Then he returned to the Underworld. After cutting the Cyclopes' chains, he took the Cyclopes to a cavern. There, they made Zeus a huge glowing thunderbolt, a powerful flash of lightning, and a deafening roar of thunder. Zeus and his followers went back into battle. Zeus's lightning and thunderbolt lit the heavens on fire. The three giants hurled rocks that made holes in the earth, and most of the Titans tumbled through them, down into the Underworld.

Zeus and his followers won the war. He and his brothers and sisters became known as the Olympian gods and goddesses. Hades became ruler of the Underworld, and Poseidon became lord of the sea. Zeus, the new ruler of the sky and king of all the gods, went to Delphi and set up the stone his father had swallowed. Then he went about choosing a bride.

Though Zeus fell in love with many women, he wanted only Hera as his royal wife. Hera did not want to marry Zeus. She knew he would not stay faithful to her.

So Zeus decided to trick her. One day, during a thunderstorm, Zeus disguised himself as a cuckoo and pretended to be hurt. Hera loved birds, so she picked up the cuckoo to comfort it. As she stroked its feathers tenderly, the cuckoo suddenly turned into Zeus. Hera fell in love with him and agreed to become his wife.

Even when Zeus had married the wife he wanted, he continued to fall in love with other beautiful goddesses, often using disguises to win them over. Hera was very jealous and argued with her husband. She could not change Zeus, so instead she punished his other loves and the children Zeus had with them.

Aphrodite and Hephaestus

One day, a pool of foam appeared on the surface of a calm sea. From this foam rose the figure of a woman. This woman was not just an ordinary woman. She was the most beautiful woman in the world. She had long, silky hair, willowy limbs, and shining eyes. Her name was Aphrodite, and this is the story of how she became a goddess.

As there was no land in sight, Aphrodite stepped daintily into a giant scallop shell and floated on the waves. Sailing along, her beauty caught the eye of Zephyros, the West Wind. He blew the scallop shell to a nearby island. When Aphrodite stepped ashore, Zephyros saw that she needed clothes to wear. He went to find the three Seasons, whose job it was to dress the gods and goddesses in elegant clothing on special occasions.

The Seasons hurried to the island to clothe Aphrodite in heavenly robes. They placed a crown upon her pretty head, a gold necklace around her milky-white neck, and sparkling bracelets around her delicate wrists. The Seasons had also brought a gold chariot with them.

"Now that you are wearing beautiful clothes and jewels, you are going to take a special journey," they told Aphrodite.

A flock of doves flew down and harnessed themselves to the chariot. Swans and sparrows, with the scallop shell in their beaks, flew Aphrodite to Mount Olympus, where the most important gods and goddesses lived.

Zeus, the king of gods, was charmed by Aphrodite's beauty. He decided she should have a place on Mount Olympus and declared her the goddess of love. He gave her a golden throne studded with precious gems. The sparrows attached the scallop shell to the back of the throne and the swans covered the throne seat with soft, white feathers. Then, the Seasons brought an embroidered cushion and placed it in front of the throne, so the new goddess could rest her feet.

Zeus, who often fell in love with beautiful goddesses, asked Aphrodite to be one of his wives. When Aphrodite laughed at his proposal, Zeus became furious.

"If you won't marry me, I will choose a husband for you," he raged. Then he called his son, Hephaestus, from his underground workshop.

Hephaestus, the blacksmith god, was the only ugly god. When he was born, his mother, Hera, had thrown him off Mount Olympus and into the sea because he was so ugly. He broke his legs in the fall and became crippled.

Aphrodite stared in dismay as Hephaestus, covered in soot from blacksmithing, limped towards her. Even though she was not attracted to him, Aphrodite knew she had to obey the king of gods.

"My son is a master craftsman," Zeus told her. "He built our palaces and homes. He made our golden thrones and all our weapons and fashioned beautiful jewelry for us to wear."

When Aphrodite heard about the jewelry, she perked up. Being married to Haphaestus might not be so bad after all. After they were married, Aphrodite persuaded her husband to make special jewelry for her. Hephaestus tried hard to keep her happy. He designed special robots to help him create golden jewelry and furniture to please Aphrodite.

Like all the gods and goddesses, Aphrodite could be very cruel if she thought somebody did not like her. Once, when the women who lived on the island of Lemnos refused to curtsy to her, Aphrodite made them smell so terrible that their husbands left them. Another time, when a man named Glaucus insulted her, Aphrodite punished him. The night before he was due to take part in a chariot race, she fed his horses some magic herbs. When the race started the next day, the horses went mad. The chariot crashed and Glaucus was killed.

Hephaestus did not approve of the things his wife did when she was angry. He wanted everyone to like her, so he made her a magical golden girdle. Whenever Aphrodite wore it, anyone who looked into her eyes fell instantly in love with her. Wearing the girdle, she looked more beautiful than ever and often had her portrait painted. So it is not surprising that Ares, the god of war, whose throne on Mount Olympus was opposite Aphrodite's, fell in love with her. They chatted and giggled together and often met secretly under a myrtle tree.

Hephaestus heard about these meetings and grew angry. He went to his workshop and made a huge net of bronze links, which he took to the myrtle tree and hung from its branches. The next time Aphrodite and Ares met there, the bronze net fell over the lovers and captured them. Hephaestus called all the other gods and goddesses to watch and laugh as Aphrodite and Ares struggled to free themselves.

Did Aphrodite ever learn her lesson? Well, she didn't stop wearing her magical girdle, so gods and princes continued to fall in love with her. But Hephaestus always forgave her. After all, Aphrodite was the goddess of love and she made sure that her husband never stopped loving her!

Apollo and the Lyre

One day, the goddess Hera heard some news that made her very angry. Her husband Zeus had another wife, named Leto, who was going to have twin babies. Hera was so jealous that she sent a dragon named Python to kill Leto. Zeus knew what Hera had done, so he ordered the wind to carry Leto away from the dragon.

After days of traveling without rest, Leto saw an island floating towards her. When she stepped onto the island, Zeus sent chains to anchor it in place. Then he commanded Poseidon, god of the sea, to raise a huge storm to hide the island from Python. The storm raged everywhere, but it stayed warm and dry on the island. There, Leto gave birth to twins, Apollo and Artemis. The babies were fed on ambrosia and nectar and grew up healthy and strong.

When the twins were fully grown, their father came down from Mount Olympus to tell them what their jobs would be. Zeus told his handsome son, Apollo, that he would be the sun god and gave him a golden chariot to carry the sun through the sky every day. Zeus told Apollo that he would also be the god of art and music. Artemis was also given special jobs of her own, including the role of moon goddess.

Zeus said to Apollo, "A fortune teller told me that one day you will play an instrument that is not yet known to gods or men. It will be called a lyre."

To show that his son was now grown, Zeus gave him a herd of cattle as a gift. He also asked Hephaestus, the blacksmith god, to make his

son a golden bow and arrows. Apollo remembered his mother's stories about the dragon that Hera had sent to kill her.

"Now that I have a golden bow, I'm going to find Python and kill her," vowed Apollo. With that, he set off over the sea to Greece.

When he reached Delphi, he heard nine wild goddesses singing. They were so beautiful that Apollo knew artists would want to paint their pictures and poets would want to write poems about them. He told them about the musical instrument that was not yet known and asked them to be his choir. The wild goddesses agreed to join Apollo, and he called them the Muses.

One day, while resting by a waterfall and dreaming of the music he and the Muses would make, Apollo heard a hissing sound. Suddenly, Python rushed out from behind some trees and charged toward Apollo. As quick as lightning, Apollo fitted an arrow to his bow, released it, and jumped aside. The arrow pierced Python's chest, and the dragon rolled down the hillside. By the time Python reached the bottom she was dead.

After that, Apollo returned home. He spent his time hunting in the forests with his sister, Artemis, and making music with the Muses. He sometimes forgot to check on the cattle that his father had given him, but there was plenty of food for the cattle in the pastures, and they did not starve.

One night, Apollo's baby half-brother, Hermes, climbed out of his cradle and went for a walk outside. Hermes was a very mischievous little boy and liked to play tricks on others. When he saw Apollo's fifty white cows in the pasture, he decided to play a joke on the god.

He tied brooms to the cows' tails and wrapped tree bark around their hooves. Strapping large bundles of sticks to his own feet, Hermes drove the cows out of the meadow. The brooms erased their tracks. The only thing left in the meadow were the strange marks made by the brooms. It looked as if a giant creature had been walking there.

The next day, Hermes sacrificed two cows to the Olympian gods. He used some of the cows' skin to make seven strings, which he stretched across an empty turtle shell. Hermes ran his fingers across the strings and the sound of music filled the air. By now, Apollo was searching for his cows. He heard the music and followed its sound. Soon he found Hermes, surrounded by his cows, making music.

"If you promise not to be angry with me for hiding your cows, I will give you this instrument I made," said Hermes.

Apollo knew that the instrument was a lyre. In exchange for the lyre, he let Hermes keep the cows.

One day when Apollo was playing the lyre, a visiting Spartan prince named Hyacinthus stopped to listen. Hyacinthus was andsome, pleasant, good at sports, and fun to be around. He and Apollo became best friends and spent lots of time together exploring forests. Apollo taught Hyacinthus how to hunt, and they often had archery contests and running races. Then Hyacinthus asked Apollo to teach him to throw the discus. Hyacinthus learned quickly. He was soon as good as Apollo and the two decided to have a discus-throwing competition.

When Zephyros, the West Wind, overheard their conversation about the contest, he had an idea. Hyacinthus had been Zephyros' best friend before he became friends with Apollo. He was jealous of Apollo's friendship with Hyacinthus and now he had a way to get back at him.

Zephyros waited until Apollo threw the heavy, metal discus. Then, Zephyros blew the discus off course. It swerved and hit Hyacinthus on the head. The prince collapsed to the ground. Apollo ran to help his friend, but he soon realized that Hyacinthus was dying from his wound.

As Apollo wept for his dying friend, his tears of grief fell to the ground and mingled with Hyacinthus's blood. Soon, a beautiful blue flower grew on that spot. Apollo named it the hyacinth and a flower called the hyacinth still grows today.

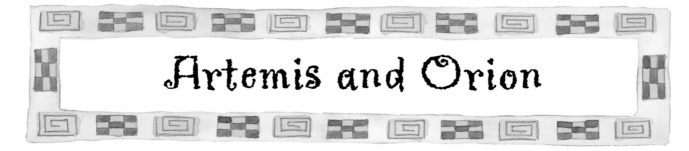

Artemis and Orion

When Zeus asked his daughter, Artemis, what she wanted for her birthday, she thought carefully and replied that she wanted a tunic with a red hem.

"Is that all?" asked Zeus. "I was going to give you a silver chariot."

"I would like a silver chariot very much," said Artemis. "I'd also like some hound dogs of my own and some nymphs to look after me. I'd like all the mountains in the world, a city, lots of jobs like my brother Apollo has. I'd also like a bow and arrows like his. Oh, and I never, ever, want to get married!"

Zeus decided his daughter would be the moon goddess. She would wear a shining crescent on her head. He made her the protector of animals and small children, the lady of the forest, and the chief hunter to the gods. He chose sixty ocean nymphs and twenty river nymphs to be her maids. Then he sent for Hephaestus, the blacksmith god.

"Take my daughter and her nymphs to the Cyclopes' forge and tell them to make Artemis a bow and a quiver full of arrows," ordered Zeus. Artemis and the nymphs set off with Hephaestus for the Island of Lipara, where fierce-looking Cyclopes, giants with only one eye in the middle of their foreheads, greeted them. But Artemis was not scared. She went close to the forge and watched while the Cyclopes fashioned a silver bow, arrows, and a quiver in which to put the arrows. Hephaestus told Artemis that no matter how many arrows she used, the quiver would never be empty.

Artemis was delighted that her birthday wishes had come true, all except one.

"What about my hounds, Father?" she asked.

"Go to Arcadia. Pan will let you choose some of his hound dogs for your own," said Zeus.

Proudly carrying her silver bow and arrows, Artemis went to see Pan, the god of nature, who was half-goat and half-man. She chose two brown and white hounds, and one spotted hound. Pan also gave her seven of his fastest hounds.

"Now," Artemis told her nymphs, "we will go and live in the forest. I'll capture four deer to pull my chariot."

Years passed, and Artemis and her nymphs lived happily in the forest. They all vowed never to fall in love and get married. They did not even talk to any men except Apollo.

Then one day, a tall and handsome hunter entered the forest with his dog, Sirius. He was Orion, the son of the ocean god, Poseidon. While resting against a tree, Orion noticed seven nymphs named the Pleiades walking down a woodland path.

Orion called out and started to run toward them. The nymphs turned around and fled, sprinting through the woods. They ran through trees and across open meadows. Orion had very strong legs, and before long, he had almost caught up with them.

The Pleiades called for Artemis to help them. Hearing their cries, the goddess changed the nymphs into white doves just as Orion was about to reach them. Higher and higher they flew, until they became seven white dots in the sky. Then, to Orion's amazement, the dots turned into a group of seven stars.

"That was very impressive," said Orion to Artemis. "Are you as good at hitting a target with your arrows?" he asked, reaching for his own bow and an arrow.

Artemis laughed and challenged Orion to an archery contest.

The contest ended in a tie. Even though Artemis had vowed never to get married, she arranged to meet Orion again the next day. The two became best friends and often hunted together. Soon Artemis did not spend much time with her twin brother.

Apollo missed his sister's company. Jealous of her friendship with Orion, he made a plan to end it forever. Apollo knew that Orion's father had given his son the power to walk on water and that Orion often waded far out to sea. The next time Orion did this, Apollo asked Artemis to walk along the seashore with him.

As they walked, Apollo boasted about how good he was at hitting a target with an arrow. He knew his sister could not resist a challenge.

"I'm just as good as you," Artemis told Apollo.

"Prove it," taunted Apollo. "See if you can hit that black dot bobbing on the waves far out at sea."

Artemis had no idea that the black dot in the distance was her friend, Orion. Confidently, she took her bow and fired an arrow. It hit its target, and the dot disappeared beneath the waves.

"There!" she said, smiling triumphantly at Apollo. Her twin smiled back slyly and waited. Eventually, the waves lifted Orion's body and carried it to the shore, where it came to rest at Artemis' feet. When she saw that her arrow had pierced Orion's heart, she wept bitterly and told Apollo she would never speak to him again.

Artemis could not bring Orion back to life, so she turned him and his faithful dog Sirius into stars. They are still around today as stars in our sky, shining just behind the Pleiades in the night.

Persephone and Hades

When Zeus and his brothers and sisters became the Olympian gods and goddesses, Hades took the Underworld as his kingdom. This meant that he owned all the precious metals and jewels in the ground. It made Hades rich, but it did not make him happy. Ruling the Underworld and all the dead was a lonely task.

Hades decided to get married so he wouldn't be lonely. He wanted a beautiful maiden named Persephone for his bride. She was Zeus and Demeter's daughter, and Zeus had once promised her to Hades.

"You'll have to trick her, though," Zeus had advised Hades. "Demeter will never agree to the marriage. She wouldn't want Persephone to live in your dark, gloomy kingdom."

Demeter was the goddess of plants and harvests. She showed people how to grow food, helped plants ripen, and helped gather the harvests. Demeter had taught Persephone everything she knew about birds, flowers, and crops. They were not only mother and daughter, but also best friends.

People were always nice to Persephone, because she was nice to them. The birds sang louder when she was near. One sunny day, Persephone wandered through a flowery meadow. Singing as she gathered roses, violets, and buttercups, Persephone weaved the blossoms into a wreath for her long, golden hair. The flowers were

so lovely that she decided to pick some more to take home to her mother.

Persephone was just heading home when she noticed a flower that she had never seen before. This unusual bloom filled the air with a wonderful perfume. How was Persephone to know that the god of the Underworld had planted this flower as a marriage trap? When Persephone knelt down to smell the flower, the ground split open. Out of the earth rode Hades in a chariot pulled by black horses. As his chariot thundered by, he scooped up Persephone.

Persephone screamed for help and Apollo, the sun god, moved the sun across the sky. Glancing down, he saw only the back of Hades' chariot as it disappeared into the ground. Apollo decided that the noise must have been one of the horses whinnying. Before long, Persephone was deep in Hades' Underworld palace. The god told her how lonely he had been. He promised to marry her and share all his riches.

"I don't want your gifts," cried Persephone. "I don't want to stay where it's dark and gloomy. I love the sun, meadows, and plants."

But it was no use. Hades was determined to make her his bride and queen of the Underworld.

Meanwhile, Demeter searched anxiously for her daughter. She scoured the hills, the meadows, the cliffs, and the seashore. She asked everyone she met if they knew where Persephone was, but nobody had seen her. Weeks passed, and all the plants and trees began to shrivel and die because Demeter was not helping them grow. She was too busy searching for her beloved daughter. One day on her travels, Demeter came across Apollo.

"Do you know where my daughter is?" she asked the god. Apollo remembered the long-ago day when he had heard a cry for help and had seen Hades' chariot disappear into the ground. He felt sorry for Demeter, who had grown old and haggard.

"I think Hades may have taken her to the Underworld," he said.

Demeter rushed to Mount Olympus and begged Zeus to force

Hades to return their daughter.

"All the plants and flowers and trees are dying," she said. "If Persephone doesn't come back to me, everything on earth will die because I won't help it grow."

Zeus knew that Demeter would carry out her threat. He agreed that Hades should return Persephone, so long as she had not eaten any food in the Underworld. Anyone who ate in the Underworld was not allowed to return to the living world.

Hades knew this. He did not want to give up his beautiful bride, so he tricked her again. Persephone had been too miserable to eat, but just before Hades released her, he persuaded her to nibble some pomegranate seeds.

"You have eaten in the Underworld!" said Hades. "You didn't eat the whole fruit, only some seeds. So for every seed you swallowed, you must spend one month here with me. The rest of the time you may spend with your mother in the living world."

When Persephone returned to her mother, Demeter was overjoyed. She became beautiful again and brought all the plants, trees, flowers, and crops back to life. When it was time for Persephone to spend her months in the Underworld, Demeter became sad and old again. Everything growing on the earth shriveled and slowly went to sleep.

The same thing still happens every year. When Persephone is in the Underworld, it is winter on earth. When she returns to Demeter, flowers and plants begin to grow again, and it is spring.

Athena and Poseidon

One of Zeus's many wives was a female Titan named Metis, who could turn herself into any creature. A fortune teller told Zeus that when Metis had children, the first child would be a daughter and the wisest of all goddesses. The second child would be a son who would be greater than Zeus himself.

"I'd like a wise daughter," said Zeus, "but not a son who will be greater than me." The fortune teller came up with a plan for how Zeus's daughter could be born, even if Metis wasn't there. She warned him that it would be painful.

Zeus tricked Metis into turning herself into a fly, and then he swallowed her. One day, months later, Zeus had a terrible headache.

He howled so loudly that Mount Olympus trembled. Hephaestus, the blacksmith god, ran from his underground workshop to see what was wrong.

"Hephaestus," ordered Zeus, "fetch an axe and split my skull open."

Zeus was immortal; this meant nothing could kill him, and any wound healed almost immediately. Hephaestus hurried to obey the order. He whirled his axe and struck Zeus on the crown of his head. The second before the wound closed, a tall, beautiful goddess sprang through the opening, wearing shining armor and carrying a spear. She was Zeus and Metis's daughter, Athena, the goddess of wisdom and war.

Although she was born fully grown, Athena had a lot to learn. Zeus sent her to Poseidon's son, Triton, a merman who lived among the dolphins with his water-nymph wife and their daughter, Pallas. Athena and Pallas quickly became best friends. Together they learned how to fish, hunt, and play games.

Like all gods and goddesses, Athena lost her temper very quickly. And like all friends, Athena and Pallas sometimes quarreled. One day, during an argument, Pallas threatened Athena with a spear. In a flash of temper, Athena snatched up her own weapon and threw it at her friend, piercing her heart and killing her.

Pallas's death filled Athena with remorse. She vowed to settle future arguments peacefully. As a tribute to Pallas, Athena said that her friend's name should be linked with her own name forever, and mortals should pray to Athena as Pallas Athena.

When Athena went back to Mount Olympus, Zeus decided that she was ready to take her place among the twelve Olympian gods.

"I should have a city of my own then," said Athena. "There's a village in Attica called Cecropia. The people there were the first to offer a sacrifice to me when I was born, so I want Cecropia to be my city."

When Poseidon heard Athena's

demand, he scowled and grumbled. As god of the ocean and almost as powerful as his brother Zeus, Poseidon controlled the waves, storms, and sea monsters. He lived in a magnificent palace beneath the sea and rode in a golden chariot pulled by white horses with bronze hooves. When he drove his chariot over the water, the storms calmed and sea monsters rose from the ocean floor and frolicked in the waves.

This power was never enough for Poseidon, though. The quarrelsome god always wanted more places to rule.

"Cecropia stands on a great rock only a little way from the sea," Poseidon said angrily. "If I strike the ground with my trident, or spear, Attica will be flooded. That will make Cecropia an island in my sea."

To prevent a fierce battle between his favorite daughter and his brother, Zeus announced a competition. He declared that whoever gave Cecropia the best gift would be the one to name it. He summoned the rest of the gods to judge the contest, and they all gathered on the flat, rocky top of Cecropia.

"It will be mine!" shouted Poseidon. He struck the rock with his trident, and at once a well of salt water appeared. The water gushed out and formed a stream, giving access to the sea. "In time, Cecropia will be a rich and powerful trading port," said Poseidon.

Then Athena stepped forward and touched the rocky soil with her spear. Immediately, a tree pushed its way through the soil. As the gods watched, the tree grew to full-size. Its trunk became thick and gnarled. Clusters of black fruit hung from the branches.

"This is the first olive tree in the world," announced Athena. "From this, other trees will grow. The olives can be eaten or crushed to make cooking oil. The oil can also be rubbed onto limbs to keep them soft."

The gods judged that Athena's olive tree was the better gift. As her reward, she called her city Athens. Poseidon was furious. He raised a huge storm that flooded Attica and formed three harbors. Although he had not intended to, Poseidon gave the people of Athens an extra gift!

Glossary

Ambrosia	The food of the gods.
Aphrodite	The goddess of love.
Apollo	The sun god; Zeus' son and Artemis' twin brother.
Arcadia	The woodland home of Pan.
Ares	The god of war; Aphrodite's lover.
Artemis	The goddess of the moon; Zeus' daughter and Apollo's twin sister.
Athena	The goddess of wisdom and war; daughter of Zeus and Metis.
Cecropia	The first name for the city of Athens.
Chariot	A two-wheeled, horse-drawn vehicle.
Cronus	The king of the Titans; Zeus' father.
Cyclopes	Giants with only one eye, in the middle of their foreheads.
Delphi	The site of the famous oracle.
Demeter	The goddess of plants and crops; Persephone's mother.
Forge	A blacksmith's workshop.
Gaia	The spirit of the earth; Zeus' grandmother.
Hades	The god of the Underworld; Zeus' brother.
Hephaestus	The blacksmith god. Zeus' ugly and crippled son and Aphrodite's husband.
Hera	The goddess of home and the family. Zeus' first wife.
Hermes	The messenger of the gods; Apollo's half brother.
Hyacinthus	A Spartan prince; Apollo's best friend.
Leto	One of Zeus' wives; mother of Artemis and Apollo.

Lyre	A stringed instrument played by Apollo.
Metis	A Titaness and one of Zeus' wives.
Mount Olympus	The home of the most important Greek gods and goddesses.
Muses	Nine goddesses who inspired art and science.
Nectar	The drink of the gods.
Nymph	A nature spirit; usually a beautiful woman.
Oracle	A place where priests gave advice or prophesy.
Orion	Poseidon's son.
Pallas	Triton's daughter and Athena's best friend.
Pan	The god of flocks and herds, half man and half goat.
Persephone	A flower maiden; daughter of Demeter and Zeus.
Pleiades	Seven nymph sisters who were changed into stars.
Poseidon	The god of the sea; Zeus' brother.
Python	A dragon sent by Hera to slay Apollo and Artemis.
Quiver	A case for holding arrows.
Rhea	The wife of Cronus.
Seasons	Three goddesses, whose job it was to clothe the gods.
Sickle	A short-handled farming tool with a semicircular blade.
Sirius	Orion's dog.
Titans	The gods who came before the Olympians.
Trident	A three-pronged spear.
Triton	A merman; Poseidon's son.
Underworld	The underground kingdom where the dead lived; ruled by Hades.
Zephyros	The West Wind.
Zeus	The king of all the gods.